PAKISTAN

EXPLORE THE COUNTRIES

Big Buddy Books
An Imprint of Abdo Publishing
www.abdopublishing.com

Julie Murray

www.abdopublishing.com

Published by Abdo Publishing, a division of ABDO, PO Box 398166, Minneapolis, Minnesota 55439.
Copyright © 2015 by Abdo Consulting Group, Inc. International copyrights reserved in all countries. No part
of this book may be reproduced in any form without written permission from the publisher. Big Buddy Books™
is a trademark and logo of Abdo Publishing.

Printed in the United States of America, North Mankato, Minnesota.
032014
092014

THIS BOOK CONTAINS
RECYCLED MATERIALS

Cover Photo: Shutterstock.
Interior Photos: ASSOCIATED PRESS (pp. 15, 17, 19, 29, 33, 35), Bloomberg via Getty Images
       (pp. 11, 25), Glow Images (pp. 13, 34), iStockphoto (pp. 5, 9, 16, 23, 34), Photothek via Getty
       Images (p. 25), Shutterstock (pp. 11, 19, 21, 27, 35, 37, 38), Time & Life Pictures/ Getty Images (p. 31).

Coordinating Series Editor: Rochelle Baltzer
Editor: Sarah Tieck
Contributing Editors: Bridget O'Brien, Marcia Zappa
Graphic Design: Adam Craven

Country population and area figures taken from the CIA World Factbook.

Library of Congress Cataloging-in-Publication Data

Murray, Julie, 1969-
  Pakistan / Julie Murray.
     pages cm. -- (Explore the countries)
  ISBN 978-1-62403-346-9
1. Pakistan--Juvenile literature. I. Title.
  DS376.9.M86 2015
  954.91--dc23
                              2013051241

PAKISTAN

CONTENTS

Around the World

Our world has many countries. Each country has beautiful land. It has its own rich history. Its people have their own languages and ways of life.

Pakistan is a country in Asia. What do you know about it? Let's learn more about this place and its story!

Did You Know?

Urdu and English are Pakistan's official languages.

The powerful Indus River flows through Pakistan.

PASSPORT TO PAKISTAN

Pakistan is in southern Asia. It borders four countries and a sea.

Pakistan's total area is 307,374 square miles (796,095 sq km). About 196.2 million people live there.

WHERE IN THE WORLD?

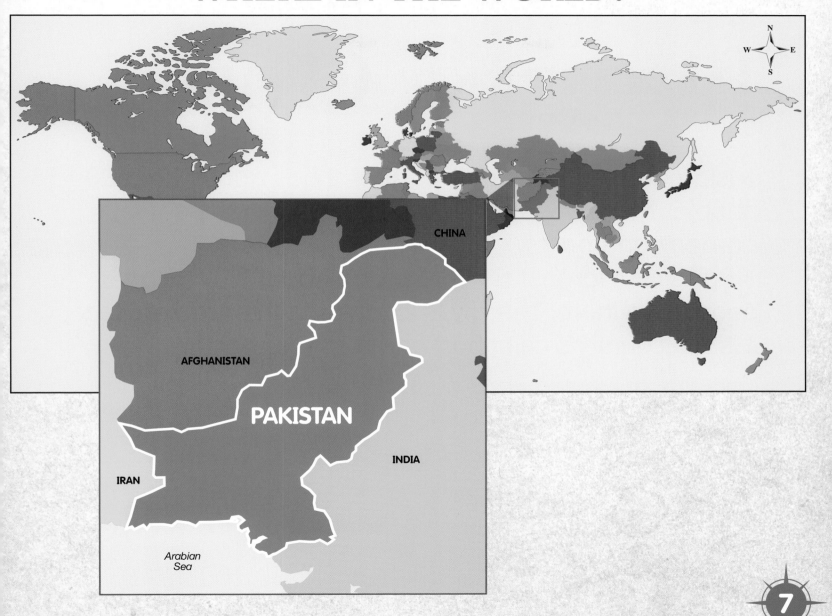

IMPORTANT CITIES

Islamabad is Pakistan's **capital**. It has about 524,500 people. This city was built in the 1960s. It has beautiful gardens and parks.

Pakistan's largest city is Karachi. About 9.3 million people live there. The city is located on the Arabian Sea. It is the country's chief port and business center.

SAY IT

Islamabad
ihs-LAH-muh-bahd

Karachi
kuh-RAH-chee

8

Islamabad is home to many government buildings.

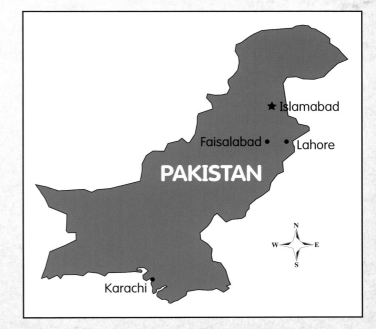

PAKISTAN

★ Islamabad

Faisalabad ● ● Lahore

Karachi

Empress Market is a famous shopping area in Karachi.

Lahore is Pakistan's second-largest city. More than 5 million people live there. It is home to weaving and milling businesses.

Faisalabad is Pakistan's third-largest city. It has about 2 million people. It is near rich land between two rivers. Wheat, cotton, and sugarcane are grown on this land.

SAY IT

Lahore
luh-HAWR

Faisalabad
feye-sah-luh-BAHD

Lahore Fort is a walled part of the city. It is more than 400 years old.

Factories in Faisalabad make products such as food and cloth.

PAKISTAN IN HISTORY

People have lived in what is now Pakistan for about 10,000 years. Around 2600 BC, they settled the valley near the Indus River. Mohenjo Daro and Harappa were their major cities.

The valley had rich land. The people grew crops such as melons, barley, and cotton. They also had tools and weapons.

Did You Know?

The people of the Indus River Valley had a written language.

Mohenjo Daro once had about 40,000 people. Today, people study the remains of this ancient city.

Over time, the land was ruled by different **empires**. In the 1800s, the British took control. In 1947, they split the land. It became Pakistan and India. Pakistan became a homeland for **Muslims**.

At first, there was East Pakistan and West Pakistan. In 1971, East Pakistan broke away. It became a new country. It was called Bangladesh. West Pakistan became Pakistan.

When the land was split in 1947, millions of Muslims moved to Pakistan.

Timeline

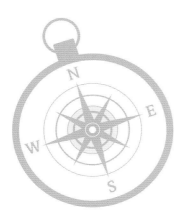

About 712

Arab **Muslims** brought Islam to the area that is now Pakistan.

1947

Pakistan and India became two nations.

1856

K2 was measured. It would be nearly 100 years before a person reached the mountain's peak.

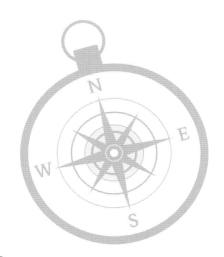

2011

Osama bin Laden was killed in Abbottabad by the US military. It is believed that he helped plan the attacks in New York City on September 11, 2001.

1959

Pakistan's government said Islamabad would be built as the **capital**.

2005

More than 73,000 people died when an **earthquake** hit north of Islamabad.

AN IMPORTANT SYMBOL

Pakistan's flag was adopted in 1947. The left side has a white rectangle. The right side is green. It has a white moon and star.

Pakistan's government is a **federal republic**. The Senate and the National Assembly make laws. The prime minister is the head of government. The president is the head of state.

The moon and star stand for Islam.

Mamnoon Hussain became president in 2013.

ACROSS THE LAND

Pakistan has mountains, deserts, and river valleys. The Himalayan mountains rise in the north. The country's highest mountain is K2.
Many villages and cities are along the Indus River. The Thar Desert borders India. A mountain pass in the north leads to Afghanistan.

Did You Know?

In January, Karachi's average high temperature is about 78°F (26°C). In June, it is about 93°F (34°C).

K2 is the world's second-highest mountain. It is 28,251 feet (8,611 m) high.

Pakistan's animals include wild boars and foxes. The mountains are home to sheep and snow leopards. Crocodiles and pythons are found in and near the rivers.

The country is home to a wide variety of plants. Pine, olive, and fruit trees grow there. There are also dry shrub forests called *rakhs*.

Did You Know?

The mostly blind Indus dolphin lives in the Indus River. Only about 1,000 remain in the world!

The markhor is Pakistan's national animal. This wild goat lives in mountain areas.

Earning a Living

Pakistan is a **developing** country. About one-fourth of the people are very poor. Some people have jobs helping visitors to the country. Others work in factories, making food or cloth.

Farming is a major business in Pakistan. Farmers grow cotton, wheat, fruit, and sugarcane. They raise cattle, chickens, and sheep. They collect shrimp, sharks, and sardines from the sea.

Pakistan's rivers provide water for crops (*above*) and for electric power (*below*).

LIFE IN PAKISTAN

Most of Pakistan's people live in the countryside. Family and community **traditions** are important to them. Many times, children live with parents and grandparents. They may also live with aunts, uncles, and cousins.

Pakistanis often eat foods made from wheat and grains. *Kheer* is a favorite dessert. Pakistanis drink sweet, milky tea and a yogurt drink called *lassi*.

Did You Know?

In Pakistan, children are not required to attend school. Because of this, many people cannot read or write.

Women in Pakistan often wear scarves called *dupattas*.

In their free time, Pakistanis go to picnics and fairs. They enjoy movies and plays. Many love to play cricket. Wrestling and horse sports are also popular.

Most Pakistanis are **Muslims**. Islam has rules about what its followers can wear and eat. People make trips to special places to honor Islam. Some children attend Islamic schools.

Eid al-Fitr is a major festival in Islam.

Muslims worship in beautiful mosques.

FAMOUS FACES

Mohammed Ali Jinnah was born on December 25, 1876, in Karachi. He became a strong Pakistani leader.

In the 1940s, Jinnah fought for Pakistan's independence. He was its first leader. He served as governor-general until his death in 1948.

People consider Jinnah the father of Pakistan.

Benazir Bhutto was born on June 21, 1953, in Karachi. She was Pakistani leader Zulfikar Ali Bhutto's daughter.

Bhutto was the country's first female prime minister. First, she served from 1988 to 1990. Then, she served from 1993 to 1996. In 2007, there was an explosion by her car. Bhutto was killed.

Bhutto was the first female leader of a Muslim country.

TOUR BOOK

Imagine traveling to Pakistan! Here are some places you could go and things you could do.

 **Play**

Splash in the Arabian Sea in Karachi. It is known for its beauty.

 **Explore**

Visit Shalimar Gardens near Lahore. These historic gardens have flowers and fountains.

 # See

Badshahi Mosque in Lahore is known for its size. It was built in the 1670s. People still pray there.

 # Eat

Try some Pakistani food. Chapati is a wheat bread. It is used to scoop up foods for eating.

 # Discover

Harappa is an ancient city along the Indus River. There, people can see the old streets and buildings.

A Great Country

The story of Pakistan is important to our world. The country is a land of towering mountains and dry deserts. It has strong roots in the **Muslim** religion.

Pakistan's people and places offer something special. They help make the world a more beautiful, interesting place.

Pakistan's cities and towns are known for their busy markets.

Pakistan Up Close

Official Name: Islamic Republic of Pakistan

Flag:

Population (rank): 196,174,380
(July 2014 est.)
(7th most-populated country)

Total Area (rank): 307,374 square miles
(36th largest country)

Capital: Islamabad

Official Language: Urdu, English

Currency: Pakistani rupee

Form of Government: Federal republic

National Anthem: "Qaumi Tarana"
(National Anthem)

IMPORTANT WORDS

capital a city where government leaders meet.

developing having few businesses and many poor people who cannot buy the things they need.

earthquake (UHRTH-kwayk) a shaking of a part of the earth.

empire a large group of states or countries under one ruler called an emperor or empress.

federal republic a form of government in which the people choose the leader. The central government and the individual states share power.

Muslim a person who practices Islam, which is a religion based on a belief in Allah as God and Muhammad as his prophet.

tradition (truh-DIH-shuhn) a belief, a custom, or a story handed down from older people to younger people.

WEBSITES

To learn more about Explore the Countries, visit **booklinks.abdopublishing.com**. These links are routinely monitored and updated to provide the most current information available.

INDEX